Linda,

Thank you so very much for bringing peace into my life and into the life of my little "Buddha Baby." We are both blessed to have you in our lives!

Much love to you —
Diane & Bennett
2008

MW00985074

peace be with you.

Compiled by Dan Zadra & Kristel Wills
Designed by Jessica Phoenix & Clarie Yam
Created by Kobi Yamada

COMPENDIUM™
INCORPORATED

live inspired.

ACKNOWLEDGEMENTS

These quotations were gathered lovingly but unscientifically over several years and/or were contributed by many friends or acquaintances. Some arrived—and survived in our files—on scraps of paper and may therefore be imperfectly worded or attributed. To the authors, contributors and original sources, our thanks, and where appropriate, our apologies. —The Editors

WITH SPECIAL THANKS TO

Jason Aldrich, Gloria Austin, Gerry Baird, Jay Baird, Neil Beaton, Josie Bissett, Laura Boro, Chris Dalke, Jim and Alyssa Darragh & Family, Tom DesLongchamp, Jennifer and Matt Ellison & Family, Rob Estes, Michael and Leianne Flynn & Family, Sarah Forster, Jennifer Hurwitz, Heidi Jones, Carol Anne Kennedy, Erik Lee, June Martin, Steve and Janet Potter & Family, Diane Roger, Kirsten and Garrett Sessions, Kelly Nolan Shafer, Heidi Yamada & Family, Justi and Tote Yamada & Family, Bob and Val Yamada, Kaz and Kristin Yamada & Family, Tai and Joy Yamada, Anne Zadra, August and Arline Zadra, and Gus and Rosie Zadra.

CREDITS

Compiled by Dan Zadra & Kristel Wills
Designed by Jessica Phoenix & Clarie Yam
Created by Kobi Yamada

ISBN: 978-1-932319-57-6

© 2008 by Compendium, Incorporated. All rights reserved. No part of this publication may be reproduced or transmitted in any form or by any means, electronic or mechanical, including photocopy, recording, or any storage and retrieval system now known or to be invented without written permission from the publisher. Contact: Compendium, Inc., 600 North 36th Street, Suite 400, Seattle, WA 98103. Peace Be With You, Compendium, live inspired and the format, design, layout and coloring used in this book are trademarks and/or trade dress of Compendium, Incorporated. This book may be ordered directly from the publisher, but please try your local bookstore first. Call us at 800-91-IDEAS or come see our full line of inspiring products at www.live-inspired.com.

1st Printing. 7500 02 08

Printed in China

Peace is not just God's gifts to His creatures.
Peace is our gift to each other.

ELIE WIESEL,
NOBEL PEACE PRIZE, 1986

Peace is our gift to each other.

"In the hearts of people everywhere there is a deep longing for peace," wrote Albert Schweitzer. A peaceful heart. A peaceful day. A peaceful life. These are worldwide yearnings—the everyday wishes of virtually all humanity—and that gives us hope.

It's hopeful to realize that there are places beyond the newspaper headlines—millions and millions of places—where people are giving each other the gift of peace and kindness at this very moment.

Travel the back roads of war-torn Muslim countries and the words *As-salaam alaykum* ("Peace be with you") will greet you at every turn. Meanwhile, millions of Catholics throughout the world turn to each other at mass and offer the words, "Peace be with you" as their gift to each other. Millions of Hindus and Buddhists daily greet each other with *Namaste* ("The divine peace in me greets the divine peace in you"). And millions of Jews say hello and good-bye with *Shalom*, the ancient Hebrew word for "Peace."

This book wishes you peace and serenity in every way. The most hopeful message of all, of course, is that you have the power to convey that message and spirit to those around you. It's been said, and it is true, that the best way to have peace in your life and in the world is to simply give it to others. As Robert Fulghum reminds us, "Peace is not something you wish for; it's something you make, something you do, something you are, and something you give away."

As-salaam alaykum. Namaste. Shalom. *Peace be with you.*

Peace begins with a smile.

MOTHER TERESA

There's a wonderful mythical law of nature
that the three things we crave most—happiness,
freedom, and peace of mind—are always
attained by giving them to someone else.

UNKNOWN

If in our daily life we can smile,
if we can be peaceful and happy,
not only we, but everyone will
profit from it. This is the most
basic kind of peace work.

THICH NHAT HAHN

Peace is not just a relationship of nations. It is a condition of the mind brought about by a serenity of soul... Lasting peace can only come to peaceful people.

JAWAHARLAL NEHRU

Nothing is more sacred than your peace of mind.

RALPH WALDO EMERSON

Do not lose your inward peace for anything whatsoever,
even if your whole world seems upset.

ST. FRANCIS DE SALES

Within you there is a stillness and sanctuary to which you can retreat at anytime and be yourself.

HERMANN HESSE

Peace does not mean to be in a place where there
is no noise, trouble or hard work. It means to be in the
midst of those things and still be calm in your heart.

UNKNOWN

At times, each of us needs to withdraw from
the cares which will not withdraw from us.

MAYA ANGELOU

Relaxation frees the heart.
Courage opens the heart.
Compassion fills the heart.

KALL

Here and there, now and then, lose yourself
in nature and find peace.

JOHN MUIR

Never lose an opportunity to see anything that is beautiful.

RALPH WALDO EMERSON

Sit outside at midnight and close your eyes;
feel the grass, the air, the space. Listen to the birds
for ten minutes at dawn. Memorize a flower.

LINDA HASSELSTROM

Let the rain kiss you. Let the rain beat
upon your head with silver liquid drops.
Let the rain sing you a lullaby.

LANGSTON HUGHES

Today I live in the quiet, joyous expectation of good.

ERNEST HOLMEN

Peace comes from feelings of satisfaction when working with joy, living with hope, loving with abandonment.

ARNOLD HUTSCHNECKER

When we seek for connection, we restore
the world to wholeness. Our seemingly separate
lives become meaningful as we discover how
truly necessary we are to each other.

MARGARET WHEATLEY

For, remember, you don't live in a world
all your own. Your brothers are here too.

ALBERT SCHWEITZER

Above all nations is humanity.

GOLDWIN SMITH

All people are my brothers and sisters,
and all things are my companion.

CHANG TSAI

Peace is not something you wish for;
it's something you make, something you do,
something you are, and something you give away!

ROBERT FULGHUM

We all have the power to give away love,
to love other people. And if we do so, we
change the kind of person we are, and
we change the kind of world we live in.

RABBI HAROLD KUSHNER

One by one we can be the better world we wish for.

KOBI YAMADA

If the world is to be healed through human efforts,
I am convinced it will be by ordinary people—
people whose love for this life is even greater than their fear.

JOANNA MACY

Love and Peace live as possibilities in us.

MARY CAROLYN RICHARDS

This I know. This I believe with all my heart. If we want a free and peaceful world, if we want to make deserts bloom and man grow to greater dignity as a human being—we can do it!

ELEANOR ROOSEVELT

In the deserts of the heart,
Let the healing Fountain start.

W.H. AUDEN

How wonderful it is that nobody need wait a single
moment before starting to improve the world.

ANNE FRANK

The first hope in our inventory—the hope
that includes and at the same time transcends
all others—must be the hope that love
is going to have the last word.

ARNOLD TOYNBEE

Love in action is the answer to every
problem in our lives and in this world.
Love in action is the force that helped
us make it to this place, and it's the
truth that will set us free.

SUSAN TAYLOR

If you want help, help others. If you want trust, trust others. If you want respect, respect others. If you want friends, be one. If you want love and peace in your life, give them away. That's how it works.

DAN ZADRA

The happiest people I have known have been those who gave themselves no concern about their own souls, but did their uttermost to mitigate the miseries of others.

ELIZABETH CADY STANTON

If we just worry about the big picture, we are powerless. So my secret is to start right away doing whatever little work I can do. I try to give joy to one person in the morning, and remove the suffering of one person in the afternoon. If you and your friends do not despise the small work, a million people will remove a lot of suffering.

SISTER CHAN KHONG

If I have been of service...
If I am inspired to reach wider
horizons of thought and action,
If I am at peace with myself,
it has been a successful day.

ALEX NOBLE

What a world this would be if we
just built bridges instead of walls.

CARLOS RAMIREZ

Unless we can hear each other singing and crying, unless we can comfort each other's failures and cheer each other's victories, we are missing out on the best that life has to offer. The only real action takes place on the bridge between people.

UNKNOWN

Blessed is the influence of one true,
loving human soul on another.

GEORGE ELIOT

Make me an instrument of peace.
Where there is hatred, let me sow love;
Where there is injury, pardon;
Where there is doubt, faith;
Where there is despair, hope;
Where there is darkness, light;
Where there is sadness, joy.

PRAYER OF ST. FRANCIS

Nothing that I can do will
change the structure of the universe.
But maybe raising my voice I can help the
greatest of all causes—goodwill among
men and peace on earth.

ALBERT EINSTEIN

If love is truly a verb, if help is a verb,
if forgiveness is a verb, if kindness is a verb,
then you can do something about it.

BETTY EADIE

The everyday kindness of the back roads more than makes up for the agony of the headlines.

CHARLES KURALT

One little person, giving all of her time
to peace, makes news. Many people, giving
some of their time, can make history.

PEACE PILGRIM

Therefore search and see if there is not some place where you may invest your humanity.

ALBERT SCHWEITZER

In every community, there is work to be done.
In every nation, there are wounds to heal.
In every heart, there is the power to do it.

MARIANNE WILLIAMSON

One is not born into the world to do
everything but to do something.

HENRY DAVID THOREAU

Do your little bit of good where you are;
it's those little bits of good put together
that overwhelm the world.

ARCHBISHOP DESMOND TUTU,
NOBEL PEACE PRIZE, 1984

Peace is not the product of terror or fear...
Peace is the generous tranquil contribution
of all to the good of all. Peace is dynamism
and generosity. It is humanity.

ÓSCAR ROMERO

One great, strong, unselfish soul in every
community could actually redeem the world.

ELBERT HUBBARD

Ordinary people often know the best ways
to approach the challenges in their own countries.
And everywhere in the world they are taking a lot
of risks by standing up and facing those challenges.

WANGARI MAATHAI,
NOBEL PEACE PRIZE, 2004

In Northern Ireland, someone had to start forgiving. Someone had to light a candle in the darkness. I thought, "Why not me?"

MAIREAD CORRIGAN,
NOBEL PEACE PRIZE, 1976

A lot of people are waiting for Martin Luther King
or Mahatma Gandhi to come back—but they are gone.
We are it. It is up to us. It is up to you.

MARIAN WRIGHT EDELMAN

I looked around and wondered
why somebody didn't do something.
Then I realized, I am somebody.

UNKNOWN

I used to pray that God would feed the hungry, or do this or that, but now I pray that He will guide me to do whatever I'm supposed to do, what I can do. I used to pray for answers, but now I'm praying for strength. I used to believe that prayer changes things, but now I know that prayer changes us—and we change things.

MOTHER TERESA

Science has made the world a neighborhood,
but it will take love to make it a sisterhood,
a brotherhood, a community of peace with justice.

ELIZABETH M. SCOTT

The love of one's country is a splendid thing.
But why should love stop at the border?

PABLO CASALS

May peace and peace and peace be everywhere.

THE UPANISHADS

People who develop the habit of thinking
of themselves as world citizens are fulfilling
the first requirement of sanity in our time.

NORMAN COUSINS

The first day or so we all pointed to
our countries. Then the third or fourth day
we were pointing to our continents. By the
fifth day we were aware of only one earth.

SULTAN BIN SALMAN AL SAUD,
SAUDI ARABIAN ASTRONAUT

In quiet places, reason abounds.

ADLAI STEVENSON

It takes solitude, under the stars, for us to be reminded of our eternal origin and our far destiny.

ARCHIBALD RUTLEDGE

Peace is every step.

THICH NHAT HANH

Peace is not the product of a victory
or a command. It has no finishing line,
no final deadline, no fixed definition of
achievement. Peace is a never-ending
process, the work of many decisions.

ÓSCAR ARIAS SÁNCHEZ

Love is the most durable power
in the world. Love is the only force capable
of transforming an enemy into a friend.

MARTIN LUTHER KING, JR.

Be a sweet melody in the great orchestration,
instead of a discordant note. The medicine this
world needs is love. Hatred must be replaced by
love, and fear by faith that love will prevail.

PEACE PILGRIM

If you want to see the brave, look at those who can forgive.

BHAGAVAD GITA

Forgiveness is the answer to the child's dream of a miracle by which that which is broken is made whole again.

DAG HAMMARSKJÖLD

People of different religions and cultures live side by side in almost every part of the world... We can reach out and love what we are, without hating what we are not. We can thrive in our own tradition, even as we learn from others, and come to respect their teachings.

KOFI ANNAN,
NOBEL PEACE PRIZE, 2001

When you reach out, the chances are pretty
good that someone will reach back.

CHERYL RICHARDSON

Peace is much more precious than
a piece of land...let there be no more wars.

ANWAR AL-SADAT

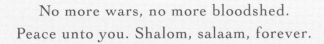

No more wars, no more bloodshed.
Peace unto you. Shalom, salaam, forever.

MENACHEM BEGIN

Person to person, moment to moment,
as we love, we change the world.

SAMAHRIA LYTE KAUFMAN

With each true friendship, we build
more firmly the foundation on which
the peace of the whole world rests.

MAHATMA GANDHI

Not all your efforts to help the world will be successful. But the worst thing that anyone can do is not to try.

JIMMY CARTER,
NOBEL PEACE PRIZE, 2002

Never to tire, never to grow cold, to be patient, sympathetic, tender; to look for the budding flower and the opening heart; to hope always, to love always—this is duty.

HENRI FRÉDÉRIC AMIEL

I wish you sunshine on your path and storms to season your journey. I wish you peace in the world in which you live and in the smallest corner of the heart where truth is kept. More I cannot wish you except perhaps love to make all the rest worthwhile.

ROBERT A. WARD